The People
vs.
The State

Using Jury Nullification To Defeat Unjust Laws

Luke von Trapp

ISBN:1982954307
ISBN-13:9781982954307

DEDICATION

To my kids S, I, K, and R: I hope one day you can live free. You are my life and the reason I do what I do. I would be lost without you all.

To A: You are my everything. Your patience during this project has been monumental and I couldn't have done this without you. I love you epically.

To Dad: I wouldn't be the man I am if it wasn't for you. We may not agree on most any topic, but I appreciate the security of knowing you always have my back.

CONTENTS

ACKNOWLEDGMENTS

I have to take a moment to thank all of our fans of Uncivil Liberty. You all have been instrumental in what we do and the people we touch.

Also, I have to thank my brothers in arms in this battle for liberty and fellow members of the Uncivil Liberty team, Halston and Horace. Our little podcast has grown into something amazing and it couldn't have been done without everything you do to make it awesome. I'm lucky to have guys like you in my corner.

1 WHY IS JURY NULLIFICATION IMPORTANT?

"The jury must judge of and try the whole case, and every part and parcel of the case, free of any dictation or authority on the part of the government. They must judge of the existence of the law; of the true exposition of the law; of the justice of the law; and of the admissibility and weight of all the evidence offered; otherwise the government will have everything its own way; the jury will be mere puppets in the hands of the government; and the trial will be, in reality, a trial by the government, and not a "trial by the country." By such trials the government will determine its own powers over the people, instead of the people's determining their own liberties against the government; and it will be an entire delusion to talk, as for centuries we have done, of the trial by jury, as a "palladium of liberty," or as any protection to the people against the oppression and tyranny of the government."

-Lysander Spooner

If you haven't heard about jury nullification, don't worry. You are not the only one.
This power held by the jury is a legal concept that is actively hidden away from the ears of the people to

prevent the people from standing up and taking control away from an overreaching government.

If you've heard about it and are not fighting for it to be implemented in our system, then something is wrong for sure. It is one of the core fundamental rights provided to us by the Constitution, and we have an obligation to use it to invalidate bad laws ratified by corrupt politicians in legislative bodies. Jury nullification is one of the rare ways to fight against the abuse of power, primarily by the law enforcement and the corrupt legal system they support.

If a jury feels a law is unjust, outdated, or immoral, the juror is permitted to "nullify" the law rather than issuing a guilty verdict. Jury nullification is a juror's way of saying, "The person before us may be guilty of the crime; however, we do not feel the law is just nor his actions criminal." Ultimately, the verdict serves as an acquittal with very little recourse, if any, from the state.

Jury nullification is one of the ways through which we can upset an oppressive system of laws that have been in place for generations. For example, the jury that is aware of racial inequalities in the system can fight against that by saying that the defendant is not guilty. If they feel the law deprives someone their right to liberty or if the law is being disproportionately applied to members of a particular community; those jurors have the power and chance to use their knowledge, their education, and their common sense to affect and improve the justice system. Each member of our society who is serving as a juror has a chance and obligation to change the person's future on trial directly and should always think twice before reaching the verdict.

Jury nullification is also one of the most important rights that we have as citizens. It gives us the power and freedom to say "no" to unjust laws. It gives us, "We The People," the final say over what kind of laws we want to be enforced. Just like the Supreme Court has the power to strike down laws, the citizen has the ability to reject laws when serving on a jury.

By implementing jury nullification, we can finally show to the public that law enforcement officers and judges are not supreme human beings, whose word we should obey without any disapproval. Through jury nullification, not only can we show that the law is equal for everyone, but we can also confirm that as a free society immoral laws have no merit and should not be enforced.

Although we are not using this right often, we need to know that it has a long history even in our country. Imagine how many ridiculous laws would be suddenly rendered obsolete, frivolous prosecutions would be avoided, and how many people would not be sitting in prison today for victimless crimes had more people known about jury nullification and not been scared to implement it.

Imagine how much lower your taxes would be if you didn't have to pay for all this nonsense. Fewer prisons, fewer judges, less law enforcement, and less wasted tax dollars.

Yes, many people were accused of committing some crime by educating others of jury nullification, yet were unable to be convicted as they were doing something that Constitution allows and protects. We can speak about this topic because it is legal to do so.

Jury nullification is undoubtedly feared just because of its ability to upset the system and reduce revenue to the state. A juror that considers drug laws to be outrageous can nullify. A juror that is aware of the mass inequality in incarceration rates and believes a defendant was targeted via racial profiling can nullify. A jury that considers a harmless defendant is a victim of the prison industrial complex rather than an actual criminal can freely nullify. Jury nullification exists so that citizens can right the wrongs inherent in our supposed "justice" system.

We need to overcome every kind of fear when it comes to the courts and the law. If we are not able to discuss our opinions and ideas freely without fear of a tyrannical response, then we don't deserve to call ourselves free citizens. If we are not prepared to stand and fight for our rights, then they are useless. It is absurd to have this right and be satisfied with not using it. Exercising one's right to nullify a law is solely a personal decision, but each juror should be made aware of their right and their power to do so.

Resources:

http://www.truth-out.org/opinion/item/23929-jury-nullification-why-every-american-needs-to-learn-this-taboo-verdict

https://www.kenneylegaldefense.us/importance-jury-nullification/

https://www.alternet.org/why-we-need-use-power-jury-nullification

https://www.copblock.org/29691/what-is-jury-nullification/

https://artvoice.com/2018/03/08/understanding-jury-nullification/#.WuJzksiFPIU

2 WHAT IS JURY NULLIFICATION?

"If a jury have not the right to judge between the government and those who disobey its laws, and resist its oppressions, the government is absolute, and the people, legally speaking, are slaves."
-Lysander Spooner

There are thousands of people in the United States who have been accused and sentenced for the crimes they haven't committed. The law is not always righteous, but in some cases, even the law cannot prevail.

What about those who are accused of breaking a law that shouldn't even be a law?

Our law libraries are crammed full of arbitrary laws placed on the books by corrupt politicians who put more importance on oppressing the people and demanding respect for their authority over the protection of rights of the individual. As the government grows, as does the countless numbers of laws. A perpetual cause and effect relationship.

How do the people fight this? Some say "Just vote better people into office to prevent this from happening..", yet we have seen this backfire numerous time, especially recently with lawmakers championing "smaller government" only to make it bigger and more oppressive. Others say "Just obey the laws like a good citizen...", however with the continual increase in laws against the people being legislated and enforced, the bubble of an individual's freedom continues to get smaller as though being involuntarily painted into a corner down the barrel of a gun only to be punished for stepping on the wet paint.

We have seen these laws continuously penalize the rights of the people. At one time interracial marriage, homosexuality, and women's right to equal treatment under the law were all illegal and considered "just", but the question is... where they actually "just", or an attempt to prevent free people from enjoying their lives to the fullest? The answer is simple.

It's 100% about control, 0% protecting the rights of the individual.

Therefore, we must ask ourselves more questions:

When the government becomes less about protecting the individual's rights and more about subjective opinions of social order, has the purpose of the law thus become null?

If the law exists only by the consent of the governed and the governed is unable to withdraw consent by other means, what recourse do the people have?

How do the people reclaim their rights when the state is continually using violence against those who act non-violently and using force to push laws that remove more rights of the people? Do we have to resort to violence or is there a more peaceful means?

When those making the law forget who they serve, the

people have no choice but to respond accordingly. If the law refuses to be just or fair, the people have an obligation and duty to override the law in the courts.

What most judges, lawyers, and politicians do not tell you is that there is a practice in our system called jury nullification. But, what is jury nullification?

"Jury nullification is a constitutional doctrine which allows jurors to acquit criminal defendants who are technically guilty, but who do not deserve punishment. It occurs in a trial when a jury reaches a verdict contrary to the judge's instructions as to the law." (CopBlock)

Simply put, the jury holds the most power in determining the validity of the law and whether it has the right to stand. Furthermore, jury nullification prevents unjust laws from being enforced even if the person standing trial has admitted to committing the "crime". It sends a message to the legislative "masters" of the people that they do not agree and refuse to convict as the law is unfit to stand. Jury nullification is a vote of non-confidence on the credibility of the law and those who profit off making these laws and the courts despise it.

Sherry Colb, a professor at Rutgers Law School, stated:

"A jury's right to decide, on a case-by-case basis, that some laws are not worthy of respect, sends the message that every law is up for grabs and that each individual is entitled to decide for himself or herself whether to follow the law. Official nullification, in other words, condones and propagates vigilantism."

Even though this doctrine is adamantly hidden away from the people by those who profit the most of the overcriminalization of activities in a "free" society, these professionals know that jury nullification is powerful. Not only that, judges use their authoritative positions to inaccurately instruct jurors to view just the facts of the case and to render their based on those metrics alone while punishing those who mention invalidating the state's edict through the jury nullification process.

Toward the end of a criminal trial, the judge will issue a set of instructions to the jurors. The judge then instructs the jury that they must ignore any personal beliefs and deliver a verdict based on the facts presented at trial solely. Sometimes juries disregard these instructions and acquit defendants who broke the law, as just one person felt this law was unjust and had no right to be enforced. The reason for this type of protected response from a juror is because they think the law itself is unjust or they think it's being unjustly levied against the defendant. At that point, the state must choose to seek an appeal or drop the case entirely.

What we all should know is that jury nullification is a discretionary act and is not a judicially sanctioned function of the jury. It is inconsistent with the will of the courts as many judges and lawyers believe that the jury's sole duty is to return a verdict based on the law and the facts of the case. However, jury verdicts the result in an acquittal are unassailable and beyond reproach even when the decision is inconsistent to the amount of evidence against the accused and a willful refusal to adhere to the instruction of the law provided by the judge. It is here where the power of the legal system falls back into the hands of the people and where change can best happen.

How come this doctrine has been practically adopted in our system when it radically opposes the law and where are its roots? To give an answer, we need to go back all way to the 18th century America. One of the oldest and most famous nullification cases is the one in 1735 in New York. It is the famous trial of John Peter Zenger, who was charged with printing seditious libels of the Governor of that colony, William Cosby. Although Zenger clearly published the alleged libels the jury still returned a verdict to "not guilty."

Outside the United States, jury nullification has an even longer history, especially in Europe, but there are many examples of this practice throughout 18th and 19th century in the United States. For instance, in medieval England, we have some cases of jury nullification dating back to the 13th century.

The power of the jury to judge the equity of the law and to invalidate laws by issuing a verdict of "not guilty" for any statute a juror felt was unjust or oppressive goes back to the signing of the Magna Carta in 1215. At the time of the Magna Carta, King John could pass any laws any time he pleased. Judges and executive officers, appointed and removed at his whim, were no more than servants of the King. This oppression became so great that the nation rose against the ruler and the barons of England compelled their king to pledge that he would punish no freeman for an infringement of any laws without the affirmation of the fact from a group of his peers.

If we go the modern era, jury nullification is most common in drug cases, where some jurors refuse to convict on possession charges either because they believe in legalization or feel that the drug laws discriminate against specific groups. Of course, we all know that in the United States there are significant differences in many states when it comes to the legalization of drugs.

Why is this so important to us? Through jury nullification, we as the people can protect the rights of others who fall victim to the overreaching governments into our individual liberties. How many cases have we seen innocent people accused of the crimes they've never committed and still convicted? Jury nullification provides one of the most peaceful ways to force change and the best ways to prevent innocent people from unjust convictions; especially when it comes to those trials where the police officers are the only evidence or the only ones who are accusing someone. It is evident that we cannot trust our current system to adequately protect our rights, reinforcing the need for jury nullification.

As stated above, one of the most significant problems we face is that most the Americans have never heard of this practice. Thanks to increased communication through internet and television, a lot of information can be passed quickly from one person to another. Even with sites like Youtube, we can send out information like this to be consumed by millions around the world.

It is important to point out that jurors cannot be punished for their decisions, even if they reached it improperly in the eyes of the court. In addition, somebody cleared of a crime as a result of jury nullification cannot be tried again for the same offense as it is a direct violation of another right that prevents double jeopardy. On the other hand, a conviction provided via nullification can be reversed on appeal to a higher court or voided by a judge depending on the jurisdiction in question. Jurors cannot be punished for "ignoring the law." They are merely bringing their decision according to what they think that is right and that is their primary argument.

We know that jury nullification has taken place in our system since the start of trials in the United States and that is why we can conclude that it continues primarily due to the way the legal system is structured. Consider it a 700-year "loophole" built inside the cornerstone of our legal doctrine and the only practical solution for a peaceful revolution to make a change in our society.

Resources:

http://www.cnn.com/2002/LAW/10/10/findlaw.analysis.colb.nullify/

https://www.copblock.org/29691/what-is-jury-nullification/

https://www.flexyourrights.org/faqs/jury-nullification/

http://www.famous-trials.com/zenger/99-nullification
http://njweedman.com/history_of_jurynullification.htm

https://www.nolo.com/legal-encyclopedia/what-jury-nullification.html

https://www.blairdefense.com/jury-nullification/

3 WHEN THE POLICE FAIL TO PROTECT THE RIGHTS OF THE PEOPLE, THE JURORS MUST

"All government, of course, is against liberty."
-H.L. Mencken

Most people aren't aware that in a Constitutional system of justice such as ours, there is a judicial body with more power than Congress, the President, or even the Supreme Court. The right to trial by jury protected under the Constitution has more power than any government official because it has the final veto power over all "acts of the legislature" that may come to be called "laws."

One of the primary concerns our founding fathers had was how to prevent the United States of America from developing an oppressive government. Much of the Bill of Rights was born out of that concern and placed rules against what government bodies cannot do, including its prohibitions on unreasonable searches and seizures, the right against self-incrimination, and the right to a trial by jury. The right to a jury trial plays a central role in our justice system and understanding its strengths, weaknesses, and function of the jury in a criminal matter is vital.

In a legal system such as ours, no one has more rights or authority over the implementation of the law than the jurors. Police officers often abuse their taxpayer-provided privileges and continually fail to protect the rights of people. When law enforcement becomes agents of revenue for the state and circumvents their responsibility to protect the people, the burden then falls on the backs of the jurors inside the legal system to correct their errors.

Under the federal civil rights statute, state and local government officials can be responsible for monetary damages on the grounds of the violation of the plaintiff's constitutional rights. However, under the color of authority, we have almost no cases against the law enforcement officers themselves, leaving the monetary burden for their improper actions to be paid by the taxpayer. If an officer makes an illegal arrest, the victim may be able to sue for a violation of his or her Fourth Amendment rights because that amendment explicitly guarantees everyone a right to be free from unreasonable seizures. Who then will arrest the police officer for his crime and his deprivation of individual rights through the use of force? Rarely do we see a legal system adequately punish their own for violations of such rights when compared to the intensity of prosecutions against non-violent criminals outside of their "club".

No matter who is sitting on the jury, they all have the same obligations. Not only are they to examine the case based on the laws, but also to protect the defendant if they think that he is not guilty or if the law is unfit to stand. As stated in the Sixth Amendment to the Constitution, this is their right and obligation. No government official can take it away from them.

In last couple years, we have seen the part of the prosecutor and the grand jury framework has undergone extreme investigation. The disappointment surrounding the ineptitude of grand juries to arraign either Officer Darren Wilson for his role in Brown's death and Staten Island Officer Daniel Pantaleo for his role in Garner's death have brought to light critical issues about the capacity of prosecutors to stay fair in cases involving local law enforcement inside the same jurisdiction. Prosecutors rely on local police to make arrests, investigate facts, interrogate suspects, and testify at trial. Police officers, in turn, rely on prosecutors to convert their arrests into convictions and assist with investigations. This type of relationship creates a very stiff conflict of interests when it comes to finding criminal justice inside the justice system.

Due to the importance of jury service, jurors should be proud to be overseeing a proper administration of the law and justice. This service is vital to preserving an existence of a government that is controlled entirely by the people. Compared to other parts of the world, our right to a trial by jury is one of our nation's fundamental and cornerstone rights that sets us apart from other countries where jury trials are only for show. These rights are preserved only when the people accept the responsibility of jury service and use it adequately. Otherwise, it serves no one.

If the police and the judges continue to degrade and unjustly pervert a legal system that is meant to protect the rights of the individual, not impose oppression upon the people, we need to preserve our power over the corruption. Given the amount of immoral and illegal activities inside the American legal system, we are left with little option to remind the legal system that the jurors are the last stronghold of justice in our country.

While we have little control over the amount of corruption inside law enforcement and the courts, it is important to remember that the people are not subject to them as though they were some aristocracy by fiat. While the people have control over publicly elected positions for executive and legislative seats, the people also control the effectiveness of bad laws. If those in power overstep their bounds and the law enforcement community refuses to disregard their instructions as an inappropriate abuse of power over the people, ultimately the validity of their tyrannical actions falls into the hands of the people as jurors.

The process can either be reversed or be reinforced. When the police refuse to protect the rights of the people, the response to this type of injustice rests solely on the people.

Resources:

http://caught.net/juror.htm

https://criminal.findlaw.com/criminal-law-basics/what-is-the-role-of-a-jury-in-a-criminal-case.html

http://www.policemag.com/channel/patrol/articles/2010/06/liability-for-failure-to-protect.aspx

https://www.nolo.com/legal-encyclopedia/defendants-rights-during-court-trial-29793.html

https://www.americanprogress.org/issues/courts/reports/2014/12/18/103578/4-ideas-that-could-begin-to-reform-the-criminal-justice-system-and-improve-police-community-relations/

http://www.ksbar.org/?juror_rights

http://www.socialstudies.org/sites/default/files/publications/se/6307/630711.html

4 IS JURY NULLIFICATION LEGAL?

"An unjust law is itself a species of violence. Arrest for its breach is more so."
— *Mahatma Gandhi*

Jury nullification is one of the best ways to fight against the oppression and misuse of power. However, one of the questions that we need to answer ourselves is one that troubles those who profit from the current legal system.

"Is jury nullification legal?"

Short answer: "Yes, it is."

In many countries around the world, including the United State, jurors have the right to nullify the law through their verdict even if the law says differently. What should prove this point even further is that from the 18th century until now we have had many cases in which jury nullification was implemented.

Confusion over whether jury nullification is legal often comes from prosecutors, judges, and other detractors who wish to discourage its use. They will often strongly imply or outright falsely state— even in the instructions to the jury—that "there is no such thing as valid jury nullification" or that to engage in jury nullification would constitute a violation of the juror's oath.

What jury nullification says to us is that people should often respect ethics, morality, and beliefs instead of made up laws. Why must the people obey some laws, when the police officers who are sworn to follow the law are allowed to break the law with no consequence? Jury nullification exists for this reason... to provide the people the ability to level the playing field against an oppressive government.

Despite the stern admonitions of the judge to "Follow these instructions," and the oath each juror takes to follow the law, juries have the raw power to ignore or change the legal rules as they apply to the evidence. First, juries are not required to explain their verdict. Unlike civil cases where juries may be asked to answer specific inquiries about their determinations, a criminal case usually results in a binary result: Guilty or not guilty. Second, even if nullification has held sway in the jury room and results in a "not guilty" verdict, the prosecution is unable to do anything about it outside of appealing the decision. Because the double jeopardy clause in the Fifth Amendment to the U.S. Constitution prevents retrial for the same crimes after one is acquitted, the accused cannot be tried again following an acquittal, regardless of any juror's rogue behavior.

Why should the jury nullification method be used more often? Let's focus on the examples where are system is making the most common mistakes. Jury nullification gives jurors an extraordinary power in confronting the racial crisis in criminal justice. It is more than evident that African Americans are frequently mistreated by our court system. If jurors think that the police are treating an African American unfairly — by engaging in racial profiling or using excessive force — they don't have to convict, even if they think the defendant is guilty. This process creates a form of "checks and balances" that echoes through the court system that the people will refuse to convict if those enforcing the law are doing so unethically.

It is also important to point out at this point that both police and prosecutors are given the same type of selective enforcement privilege, allowing them to pick and choose which laws to enforce. If more juries flex the will of the people and refuse to convict, law enforcement and the state will be less ambitious in arresting and accusing someone of a crime because of a lack of support of the people needed to convict.

This potential to force a change in the system is the main reason why jurors need to be encouraged to say "no" to the system. If they think that a law is wrong, they have a right and power to say that. The people have a reason to be angry for many things, but still, we need to believe that the jurors are those who will invalidate the bad laws that the legislative masters continually subject the people to.

In almost 20 years, there are just two jurors that have been prosecuted for their verdicts. Both prosecutions failed, and the courts upheld the long-standing tenet of our legal system that jurors cannot be punished for their conclusions.

This means that jurors cannot be formally rebuffed for their decisions and the danger of punishment in the form of having to deal with legal repercussions is extremely low, even for jurors who openly discuss matters relating to jury nullification and concerns of conscience. In many scenarios where the prosecutors have too much power in their hands, the jurors are the only people who have a chance to change the situation.

Jury nullification gets far too little respect, primarily due to the propaganda that floods our legal system that it is illegal or ineffective when in actuality it is neither. Though it is apparently within the rights of the jurors to refuse to convict whenever they choose, judges and prosecutors often view this practice with extreme hostility as it gives too much control to the people. They may not be able to stop juries from exercising their power over the court, but they do their best to shield individuals from educating the jurors that they have this option.

One key argument by those in favor jury nullification is pointing out that a trial by our peers is guaranteed because we want decisions to be levied by the common sense of lay people, not the aristocracy of government employees. In a way, the jury is the conscience of society. Their job is not only to decide whether the defendant did the acts charged, but whether the law is just and if someone should be punished for it. The actions and powers of the jury protect us from immoral or socially undesirable results.

Jurors need to be educated that they can say no if they so choose, as Paul Butler wrote in his article:

"If you are ever on a jury in a marijuana case, I recommend that you vote "not guilty" — even if you think the defendant actually smoked pot or sold it to another consenting adult. As a juror, you have this power under the Bill of Rights; if you exercise it, you become part of a proud tradition of American jurors who helped make our laws fairer."

Resources:

http://fija.org/document-library/jury-nullification-faq/is-jury-nullification-legal/

https://www.lawyers.com/legal-info/criminal/criminal-law-basics/jury-nullification-when-the-jury-ignores-the-law.html

https://www.washingtonpost.com/news/in-theory/wp/2016/04/05/jurors-need-to-take-the-law-into-their-own-hands/?utm_term=.d65c149e66b0

http://fija.org/2014/09/15/jury-myths-and-misconceptions-can-jurors-be-punished-for-jury-nullification-verdicts/

https://www.washingtonpost.com/news/in-theory/wp/2016/04/06/prosecutors-have-too-much-power-juries-should-rein-them-in/?utm_term=.656008a7a75d

https://www.nytimes.com/2011/12/21/opinion/jurors-can-say-no.html

5 BAD LAWS DESERVE TO BE BROKEN

"That which is not just is not law."
— William Lloyd Garrison

Martin Luther King once declared, "*I would be the first to advocate obeying just laws. One has not only a legal but a moral responsibility to obey just laws. Conversely, one has a moral responsibility to disobey unjust laws. I would agree with St. Augustine that "an unjust law is no law at all."*

This idea is something that was spoken more than fifty years, yet it looks like we still haven't understood the real meaning of these words. It is apparent as we still have corrupt enforcement of the laws, abuses of privilege and tyrannical leaders in official ranks. There is always someone who should protect the law, but instead is the first one to break it. But, how can we change things? Well, firstly, by not allowing bad laws to be implemented. If we are aware that some statutes are unjustified, we need to speak up and fight against them. Jury nullification is a powerful way to use more than words to spark change in the legal system.

Many people will advocate that one should rely solely on the legislature to remedy immoral laws they place on the books for the people to follow. This type of logical fallacy puts the burden of honesty and integrity enforcement on the same people who actively engaged in the process of creating similar unjust laws. Because of this breakdown in logic, we have seen immoral and unjust laws not only be forced upon the shoulders of the people, but also fervent enforcement of these laws driven by hate for those on the other end of the equation. For example, laws that prohibited the interracial marriages were levied against the people and strictly enforced. Were these laws just? Were they moral? The main reason these laws stayed in existence for as long as they did rest mainly in the logical fallacy that the legislators and judges were the only ones able to invalidate laws. This mentality bypassed the individual jurors responsibly to act in the best interest of the individual on trial and the validity of the law as it is applied to society, instead of using the weak excuse that a juror can only judge the facts.

For the record, U.S. anti-miscegenation laws restricting marriages, on the base of race, were once enforced in most states. In the 1660s, Maryland became the first colony to prohibit interracial marriages. By 1967, over 15 states still had anti-miscegenation laws still being enforced by the state. All were in the southeastern United States, from Virginia to Texas to Florida; however, the territories of Alaska and Hawaii and a few other states in the Northeastern U.S. never passed these types of anti-miscegenation laws. The legislatures of other states repealed their laws at various times, but the overall excuse that depriving individual the right to marry and love who they choose was a societal norm across the United States in itself is a fallacy.

Disobedience to bad laws is vital, and processes like jury nullification can jolt democratic processes into motion. The question remaining is when we should disobey the laws. This question has regularly propelled men into a radical examination of the premises of personal morality and civic obligation and, indeed, of government itself. While the philosophical implications pose a large number of questions, it has always been a painfully practical question as well.

The laws need to be changed, and we cannot rely on our elected politicians to protect our freedom and liberties. If the legislators and judiciary refuse to protect individuals and their rights, the people have no other option but to defend them through nullifying the law through jury service. If the people do not see reforms in that field, the only solution would be to oppose the law in every way possible. If the people refuse to stand opposed to overreaches from government into areas it has no authority to operate in, we continuously lose the battle to protect our rights from tyrants who seek to remove them "for the greater good".

Our disobedience shows that we take our rights and obligations seriously and are aware that the people hold the ultimate authority over government. We need remember that the people are within their individual rights and moral obligation to do so, displaying civil disobedience when we realize that something is wrong with the system. We have also to realize that the law enforcement officers and judges will not and can not be relied upon to protect us. If the people fail to disobey unjust laws, they are just as culpable for their existence as the ones who make them and enforce them.

Criminal laws are created to further the state's authority over the people by means of compliance. The power over the people can be advanced only if members of society fail to comply. These criminal laws are designed to be followed without question and with total subjection to implied authority. Other laws and regulations are not created with compliance in mind, but rather the revenue it could potentially bring to the state. Conviction, in these cases, is no regrettable fallback.

We should continuously stress that there are laws that should not be followed. If we throw them out, we will be able to say that the system is functioning correctly. The only way for the people to discard bad laws directly and peacefully is through actions like jury nullification.

In some states, the punishments for non-violent offenses are so severe that lives of people are destroyed. Outrageously long sentences and unjust penalties are only part of the story. Thousands of people are arrested each year for minor, non-violent offenses,yet do not go to jail, also suffer from the stigma placed upon having a record. Their arrests and involvement on the wrong side of the legal system stay on their records for years which cripple their prospects for jobs, loans, housing, and benefits. Often these are disproportionately minorities, with marijuana criminalization hitting black communities the hardest.

What we are talking about is justice. Justice for the people who fund and control the governmental system we have today. How can we even discuss something if we are not willing to change the things that are wrong? How can we talk about bad laws if we are not prepared to stand against them? We have an obligation to ourselves and others around us to ensure we prevent rights from being removed from the people. We must be the ones who are creating and changing the country we live in and all the laws that are placed upon us. If our leaders are opposing our fundamental human rights, why should we blindly obey them?

Lack of action is an affirming action, in and of itself.

Resources:

http://www.slate.com/articles/life/longform/2014/10/mlk_s_letter_from_a_birmingham_jail_and_other_great_open_letters.html

http://www.religioustolerance.org/hom_mar14.htm

https://www.nytimes.com/1964/01/12/is-it-right-to-break-the-law.html

https://link.springer.com/article/10.1007/s11572-017-9442-9

https://www.nytimes.com/2014/07/29/opinion/high-time-the-injustice-of-marijuana-arrests.html

.

6 THE COURTS HATE THE FIRST AMENDMENT

"Whoever fights monsters should see to it that in the process he does not become a monster. And if you gaze long enough into an abyss, the abyss will gaze back into you."
— Friedrich Nietzsche

Our legal system has many flaws, and these flaws are more than evident.

One of the main reason for that is our ignorance of our rights that are guaranteed by the Constitution.

Jury nullification is a prime example. Jury nullification occurs when a jury acquits the defendant, despite the evidence, because they either believe the law is immoral or wrongfully applied. Although many may think that telling jurors about jury nullification is illegal, that is simply not true. The main problem is that those who are implementing the laws have a significant problem with this issue, mainly the judges and the prosecution.

One would think that of any place that would respect one's First Amendment right to freedom of speech, the courtroom would be the place where one could exercise this right. However, the courts are the primary arena where one's right to speak freely and provide themselves a proper defense is heavily stifled. There are too many cases in which we can see that the judges are violating the first amendment by not allowing people to speak their mind about topics that do not support their fiat control over the justice system.

Of course, this kind of interpretation comes from the fact that in the traditional approach jurors are triers of fact, while the judge is considered as the interpreter of law and the one that will instruct the jury on the applicable law. Ironically, the jurors have a right to disregard a judge's instruction and provide their verdict based not only on the facts, but they also can issue a verdict based on the credibility of laws that oppress the people. Jurors do not need to be afraid, as the law, in this case, is defending them.

It is critical to remember that first amendment states very clearly :

"Congress shall make no law respecting an establishment of religion or prohibiting the free exercise thereof, or abridging the freedom of speech, or of the press; or the right of the people peaceably to assemble, and to petition the government for a redress of grievances."

Given that Congress, by definition, is the only body able to pass laws and regulations at the Federal level and that amendments to the Constitution are superior to arbitrary internal codes of conduct and draconian regulations; the courts have no legal authority to prevent freedom of speech from being exercised. In this case, since the this is a Constitutional right that is protected against actions of the state, courts who allow freedom of speech to be hampered are in direct violation of the Constitution they are required to protect.

Nevertheless, sometimes the first amendment can be intentionally misinterpreted to protect the court's perception of ultimate authority over the people. A prime example of judicial overreach happened in 2015 in Denver, when two men were charged with seven felony counts each for handing out FIJA (Fully Informed Jury Association, an organization that spearheads jury nullification advocacy) brochures as jurors were entering the courthouse. Since then, federal courts have granted and upheld a preliminary injunction against any further such arrests because this is First Amendment-protected activity. State courts have also thrown out all the charges against the two juror rights educators because their activity was legal and protected speech under the First Amendment.

A similar thing happened to Keith Wood who was arrested and charged with jury tampering (misdemeanor) and obstruction of justice (felony). The pamphlets Wood handed out specifically discussed a jurors' right to vote their conscience, known as jury nullification of law. We can mention a dozen of similar cases, but we will stick to these two because they are showing the point.

In both cases we have the same question "Is handing out flyers outside a courthouse and educating people about jury nullification protected by the First Amendment?"

Courts have ruled against themselves multiple times, and the answer is, "Yes, it is."

Even though jury nullification and the educating of people about jury nullification is a protected activity under the first amendment, judges and police officers try to scare jurors into believing their misrepresentation of the role of a juror. Instead of being honest and truthful with jurors and allowing them to be fully informed of their rights under the Constitution, they attempt to scare jurors into submitting to their pseudo-authority by stating that voting on the validity of the law is an illegal act. The only problem is that ideas about free speech sometimes doesn't compute in the age of social media.

Fighting to educate people about the right of jury nullification is an act of protecting the rights that are protected by the first amendment. Failure to do so allows an oppressive judicial system to continue destroying the lives of those who are only guilty of going against the opinions of the state and the judges. Our legislative, judicial, and law enforcement communities have proven multiple times that they cannot be trusted to be honest and fair in their dealings with the people; therefore, the people must work against them to ensure rights are adequately preserved.

As Wood's attorney, David Kallman, said after the trial, "The prosecutors made it clear, they are not going to back off. They will arrest someone next week for the same thing. So, they need to be stopped. You can't squelch people's rights to hand out information just because you don't like it."

Proponents of nullification have long argued that the power of the jury to refuse to convict presents a vital check against tyrannical or overzealous government. However, some courts have reasoned that a nullification instruction would permit and potentially encourage the jurors to disregard the law in its entirety or allow them to break the law as they see fit. One court even opined that it is proper to affirmatively (and erroneously) inform the jurors that they would "violate the law" if they advocated and practiced jury nullification, or if they violated any of the judge's instructions on the law.

Of course, there are always two sides of the story. In general, there is still one truth.

Given the current behavior and lack of constitutional common sense, the judges continually fail in their protection of first amendment rights in their courtrooms. Together with law enforcement officials, the courts try to challenge and squash the first amendment but eventually will fail. Why? Because citizens will stand against them and many will fight to protect their freedom of speech and prevent oppression from their elected leaders.

Jury nullification has existed since the beginning of the trial system and persists because of the purveying number of potential flaws in the legal system that are supposedly designed to protect the integrity of the jury process. The law also limits the court's capacity to investigate the jurors' motivation or intent during or after a verdict. By law, jurors cannot be punished for their verdict, even if the courts feel they reached it improperly. Also, someone acquitted because of jury nullification cannot be tried again for the same crime because of the prohibition against double jeopardy. The ultimate power of the criminal process lies in the hands of the jurors, and the legal system fights tirelessly to ensure the ignorance of the people they are sworn to protect through misinformation and half-truths.

Resources:

http://legal-dictionary.thefreedictionary.com/Jury+nullification

https://www.law.cornell.edu/constitution/first_amendment

https://www.quora.com/Why-is-telling-jurors-about-jury-nullification-illegal-but-its-legal-when-used-by-jurors-Isn%E2%80%99t-it-possible-that-a-juror-may-actually-know-about-jury-nullification-beforehand

https://www.usnews.com/news/articles/2016-03-25/judge-dismisses-felony-against-jury-nullification-evangelist

http://fox17online.com/2015/12/01/man-charged-with-felony-for-passing-out-fliers-in-front-of-courthouse/comment-page-1/

https://scholarship.law.georgetown.edu/cgi/viewcontent.cgi?referer=https://www.google.com/&httpsredir=1&article=2842&context=facpub

http://constitution.org/2ll/2ndschol/131jur.pdf

https://www.nolo.com/legal-encyclopedia/what-jury-nullification.html

7 JURORS: THE LAST HOPE FOR OPPOSING TYRANNY

"I became convinced that noncooperation with evil is as much a moral obligation as is cooperation with good."

— Martin Luther King Jr.

The oppression by lawmakers is something that is ever present in our daily lives. Nevertheless, one of the things that we must strive to ensure is fighting against that oppression as peaceful as possible. The easiest and most effective ways to do that is by flexing our legal rights as the people, and the best chance to do this is through jury nullification.

Although most of the people think that the primary role of the jurors is to dispense punishments to fellow citizens accused of breaking various laws, the real truth is that their foremost obligation is to protect those same citizens from tyrannical abuses of power by government. The Constitution is extremely vocal about the right of trial by jury and the ultimate power the jury has. The importance placed on the power of a trial by jury means that the government must not only bring its case before the jury of the people but must also prove the validity of the laws over a society if that same government seeks to deprive any person of life, liberty or property. Jurors have the unique right to reject a law and oppose government tyranny by refusing to convict.

As Thomas Jefferson said:"I consider trial by jury as the only anchor yet imagined by man, by which a government can be held to the principles of its constitution".

Many groups in this country feel the government has overstepped its power in some way and circumvented the rights of the people in such a way that there must be protection for the natural rights of citizens against the continuous overreach at both state and federal levels. These groups are not only defending the right to protest, carry a gun, or not wear seatbelts but challenging the authority of the government to decide such matters without the mediating effect of a jury's judgment of fairness in those cases. All people, regardless of political alignment, should actively defend those principles which proves why we must have full trust in the education of our jurors. Of course, we all expect that they will return us that favor by doing their job in the best possible manner.

If you are serving as a juror, you need to know all the rights and duties that come with that responsibility. Firstly, a juror can stop the government cold if he believes the statute to be unconstitutional or unfair by merely voting not guilty. When a jury at the end finds a defendant not guilty in the cases where he did violate the statute, and the evidence is clear to that fact, it nullifies the statute in that case. The more cases that result in no convictions, the less likely the law is to be enforced and prosecuted, as it shows there is little to no interest from the people to continue enforcement of an obsolete law.

It is at this point where the juror, in effect, acts as judge and jury of not only the criminal justice system but also of the legislative branch of the government. When laws are no longer able to be enforced, they become just words on paper with no tangible value and are removed or replaced more sensible laws that are in-line with the will of the people.

It is also important to mention that the lawyers and the judges will always try to misinterpret the strength of the jurors and their rights, but even they know that the power of the jurors in the courtroom is immeasurable and the courts answer only to the individual who holds power, the juror. In criminal cases, one lone juror holds the power to prevent an unjust conviction. The right to trial by jury represents one of the loudest and peacefully powerful checks against the tyranny of government. The jury is there, by design, "to prevent oppression by the Government" and to "protect against unfounded criminal charges brought to eliminate enemies and against judges too responsive to the voice of higher authority."

The power of jury nullification was more prevalent in the early years of the United States, inspiring minds like Lysander Spooner to write "*For more than six hundred years - that is, since Magna Carta, in 1215 - there has been no clearer principle of English or American constitutional law, than that, in criminal cases, it is not only the right and duty of juries to judge what are the facts, what is the law, and what was the moral intent of the accused; but that it is also their right, and their primary and paramount duty, to judge of the justice of the law, and to hold all laws invalid, that are, in their opinion, unjust or oppressive, and all persons guiltless in violating, or resisting the execution of, such laws.*"

What we can quickly conclude is that jurors in our criminal justice system have more rights than we are aware of, an involuntary ignorance that is crafted by design. If these rights were exercised on daily basis, the constitutional rights that we as a people claim to treasure would not be as abused as they are today. Not only are individual rights guaranteed inside the verbiage of the constitution, individuals also possess natural rights that must also be protected just as intensely by those in power. If the lawmakers we elect to represent the people refuse to defend the rights of the same people, then the people have little choice in expressing their authority over their government officials.

Without actively fighting the tyranny of the government, we will never be able to say for ourselves that we are free citizens in this, or any, country. If people say they believe in liberty, are we willing and able to defend our freedoms? No one can limit our rights without our approval as a government does not give rights; however, they are protected by the documents that formed this country 200 years ago. These are the documents and protections upon which the foundation of which a whole nation lies.

The people that came before us and many of our ancestors fought for independence from tyranny in many forms. Even the Declaration of Independence states: "when a long train of abuses and usurpations, pursuing invariably the same Object evinces a design to reduce them under absolute Despotism, it is their right, it is their duty, to throw off such Government, and to provide new Guards for their future security…"

Our right and obligation is to protect our liberty at all costs, not bow and scrape to the whims of elected officials who claim authority over a presumed "free people". We can do that only if we are able to respect ourselves enough to flex the rights built into our justice system upon the founding of a government such as ours.

Let us not forget that one juror's voice can hold more power than a room full of soldiers as the armed forces of the state are quick to obey their own edicts. That power is to be exercised as it can change the course of our lives and beliefs. Without it, we can only watch law enforcement and the legal system abuse their powers without anyone opposing to them. These corrupting powers will continue this level of malfeasance only if we allow them to.

Jury nullification allows every person to oppose that tyranny in a non-violent manner and to show that a united people can remind oppressive leaders, especially to those who profit off the mistreatment of the people. The people control the courts and thus, the law itself.

Resources:

http://fija.org/

http://www.freedom-central.net/trialbyjury.html

http://prorev.com/juries.htm

http://webpages.charter.net/mad_prophet/articles/jurors/stump.ht
ml

http://constitution.org/2ll/2ndschol/131jur.pdf

http://webpages.charter.net/mad_prophet/articles/jurors/stump.ht
ml

http://www.ushistory.org/Declaration/document/

8 POLICE WON'T ENFORCE LAWS THAT DON'T GET CONVICTIONS

"The police have lost sight of the fact that they are public servants."
— Steven Magee

Most of the police work today is reactive and incident-focused rather than proactive and strategic. Efforts to shift policing towards a more effective and sustainable approach to crime reduction have been few and far between. According to statistics around one-third of homicide in the United States are unsolved. To put this into perspective, just fifty years ago this rate was more than 90 percent. Basically, every third murder in the states is left unsolved. But why is that so? Why do numbers are saying that the efficiency of the police has never been lower?

In many cases police officers are not willing to do their job, especially if they are not sure that the case will be solved. It is easier to go after low hanging fruit where convictions are easy instead of those unsolved violent crimes where administrators believe that such a pursuit would be just a waste of money and resources. With this mentality, it is easy to see why non-violent and arbitrary laws are being enforced at a higher level as it is an easy win and gives a quick ROI for law enforcement budgets.

According to research done by USA TODAY, police and prosecutors are allowing tens of thousands of wanted felons — including more than 3,300 people accused of sexual assaults, robberies, and homicides — to escape justice merely by crossing a state border.

The numbers are astonishing. This clearly show us that police officers are not effectively using their resources, like pursuing crimes against people and property. Millions of dollars are being spent, and still, there are thousands of unsolved crimes.

According to other research, police and prosecutors generated more than $17.8 million in forfeiture revenue from 2009 to 2016. Nearly two-thirds of those proceeds came from civil forfeiture cases, where the owner did not have to be convicted. Law enforcement predominantly confiscated cash but also seized dirt bikes, gold chains, and electronics like iPads, TVs and cell phones without court order and sold these items at auction to generate revenue for law enforcement bonuses and activities. It appears that taxpayer-funded law enforcement officials are allowed to take our money as they want and spend it as they see fit, but they can't use that money to solve the severe crimes that are surrounding us. Combine that with the fact that low-level, non-violent crimes are easier to convict than violent crimes; we can easily argue that resources are "best" spent criminalizing one's natural right that harms no one than it is the mountains of unsolved violent and fraudulent crimes against the people.

We need to ask ourselves if it is more important to have a law enforcement industry that pursues violent criminals or one that wastes money on convicting and housing victimless "criminals".Since law enforcement often goes for the low hanging fruit when it comes violators of arbitrary and even draconian laws that have no real victim, how do we stop that without having to rewrite the entire system of laws we are governed by? These types of questions have answers rooted in jury nullification.

In a Washington Post article, Yale Law School Professor Stephen Carter admitted that he counsels his first-year students "...never to support a law they are not willing to kill to enforce. Usually, they greet this advice with something between skepticism and puzzlement, until I remind them that the police go armed to enforce the will of the state, and if you resist, they might kill you." If their job is to "serve and protect", should they do that no matter how hard the obstacles are? If the law is same for all of us, why is it not implemented in every single case? The current state of the criminal justice system has to do with the fact that for law enforcement and the courts to maintain relevance for continued taxpayer funding, they need people to arrest and convict to establish some level of need of their services.

If the juries are no longer willing to convict on charges of victimless crimes (like marijuana users, for example), the taxpayers will begin to notice that their funds are consistently squandered on trials lacking adequate results. Combine that with the fact that many high-level prosecutor positions are elected positions with kooshy salaries and benefits (and in some cases, senior law enforcement jobs as well), in order to maintain their position and relevancy to the voter base, they are then required pursue other, more difficult crimes, to get the convictions they need for their resumes.

Fortunately, some police departments are now feeling the pressure to reverse this trend. Detroit is an extreme case. When the city was on the verge of bankruptcy, the murder clearance rate was flirting with single digits. A new chief was brought in, and homicide investigators were reorganized into squads that "specialize" in certain parts of the city. Cities such as Detroit are also trying to improve their clearance rates by digging into their files, looking for older cases that might be able to be solved with new techniques. During this time, focus on minor victimless crimes was no longer an importance. This shift in policy back to enforcing laws where there were actual victims allowed the police department to regain some level of credibility in the eyes of the taxpayers.

Ideally, this type of focus should be every law enforcement officer's priority, but what happens when there are more police officers than the jurisdiction requires to manage violent crimes? What do you do with bored law enforcement who go out "looking" for some law to be broken? In these situations, you have LEOs who go out of their way to justify their position by creating a violation of a law where there is none. In some cases, municipalities will create more arbitrary laws to prove the importance and the need for these law enforcement officers. Instead of repurposing these officers to other roles inside the structure of government, they are sent to go after violators of new victimless statutes to keep the supply of people running through the legal system, artificially validating their role in society.

Once we position our legal system in such a way where the people utilize jury nullification to check not only the judicial system but also the legislative system; we will then begin to see a change in the way law enforcement does their job. If these officials realize that the people no longer want their resources wasted on violators of arbitrary statutes but instead focused on those who commit violence and fraudulent acts against members of the society, their priorities will be forced to change if they wish to preserve their revenue stream and position inside the taxpayer-funded governmental structure.

Using jury nullification in these matters reminds everyone in the governmental hierarchy that the people are the ultimate authority and each position answers directly to the people in the way or another. If the courts, through jury nullification, are unable to convict because the people no longer have confidence in the laws they are supposed to enforce, then the laws are no longer enforceable and become irrelevant. The jurors, not the actors inside the system, are vital for forcing a change in a corrupted system.

Resources:

http://www.police-foundation.org.uk/uploads/holding/projects/policing_and_crime_reduction.pdf

https://www.npr.org/2015/03/30/395069137/open-cases-why-one-third-of-murders-in-america-go-unresolved

https://www.usatoday.com/story/news/nation/2014/03/11/fugitives-next-door/6262719/

https://www.forbes.com/sites/instituteforjustice/2017/07/11/connecticut-just-banned-civil-forfeiture-without-a-criminal-conviction/#771678ab52e7

https://www.washingtonpost.com/news/volokh-conspiracy/wp/2014/12/05/dont-support-laws-you-are-not-willing-to-kill-to-enforce/?utm_term=.ec2feafefb4a

https://www.npr.org/2015/03/30/395069137/open-cases-why-one-third-of-murders-in-america-go-unresolved

https://www.quora.com/What-options-do-you-have-if-the-police-refuse-to-enforce-the-law

9 REMINDING THE COURTS WHO IS ACTUALLY IN CHARGE

"Power does not corrupt. Fear corrupts... perhaps the fear of a loss of power."
— *John Steinbeck*

The instructions to a jury from a judge in a United States court frequently is more than a statement of the rules of law, and it may contain a summary of the facts or some of the points of a case. The juror must reach their own conclusion whether based on the evidence presented or on the validity of the law itself. The juror is allowed to enter their verdict without regard to what may be the opinion of the judge as to the facts. The judge will often point out and explain what the disputed facts are and what circumstances may not matter in the case at hand. In other words, the judge may try to direct the jury's attention to the real merits of the case and impartially summarize the evidence bearing on the questions of fact. The judge will state the law related to the facts presented to the jury.

Nevertheless, the jurors are those who have the final word. The jury is in charge as they are deciding if someone guilty or not. The people, not the judges, have the supremacy in making the final decision.

Jurors have a right to ask for and receive all items received into evidence by either side, the jury instructions themselves, and any notes taken by the jurors during the trial. Once the case has been heard and is submitted, the jury is kept together under the supervision of a court officer to render their verdict.

Jurors should give close attention to the testimony, but also the credibility of the law that is forced upon the people without consent. They are sworn to disregard their prejudices and must render a verdict according to their best judgment. Each juror must keep an open mind while voting their conscience. Logic dictates that when dealing with the psychology of society, once a person comes to a preliminary conclusion regarding the facts placed before them, they are less likely to change their views unless there is ample reason to do so. Therefore, it is wise for jurors not even to attempt to form an opinion on the facts of the case until all the evidence has been clearly presented to them and deliberation begins. Similarly, jurors are not to engage in discussion among themselves until the case is concluded.

After they fulfill all these necessities, the jurors are ready to bring the right decisions. Law enforcement officers and judges are frequently biased thus making the jurors the sole voice of reason in the legal process. Because a juror's power is almost absolute, they have the ability to reverse the law in every criminal case and make the right choice based not only on the facts and the law but also on the morality of the law and if it is fit to be applied.

Jury service is one of the most important exercises of civic obligation and a valuable privilege that provides the juror the reminder that they ultimately control the system, as one opposing voice can provide a complete shutdown of the current trial. There is no more vital work a citizen can perform in the exercise of self-government than honest and conscientious jury service. Service as a juror carries more weight than that of the judge, and every juror should appreciate the way that an essential obligation has been performed. Indeed, the viability of our system of justice is calculated by the enthusiasm and devotion in which the members of the jury govern our courts.

How many times have we heard that the law enforcement officers arrest someone without clear evidence? How many times have we seen illegal activities from taxpayer-funded officials cause undue harm to a person of the citizenry? Without juries and the power they hold, many of these "criminals" would have no chance to escape the clutches of an oppressive legal system. Many are found guilty without the proper reason but, even with these errors, the jurors have managed to create a more effective system when compared to the alternative. Without them, a justice system would be entirely for show in the modern day political theater.

On appeal, the defendant can raise claims that mistakes were made in applying and interpreting the law during the trial. The defendant may assert that the judge illegally admitted hearsay testimony into the proceedings, gave improper or inaccurate jury instructions, or should not have permitted the prosecution to use evidence obtained in violation of the defendant's constitutional rights. If the appellate court agrees that there were significant errors in the trial, the defendant will get a new trial. In the case, if the jurors have made some mistake, another jury has a chance to correct it. This peer-review methodology is another privilege afforded the people that should not be taken for granted.

Through this, we can conclude that the jurors have not only a constitutional right to bring the most important decisions but also the obligation to exercise a "checks and balances" system against the courts and ultimately, the legislators. In the courtroom jurors are the ones that are in charge and no one, including the judges, cannot oppose to what they conclude. Jurors can make a mistake; however, what is essential that the conclusion they made represented their own will and that decision was one not made through threat of force. Judges are often conceited and believe that the courtroom is their playground where they make all the calls, and that is correct up to a point. However, the verdict and the future of the person standing trial rests solely in the hands of the juror.

If the juror has all the information about his role in this process, there is practically no room for mistakes. Unfortunately, the juror rarely has all the correct knowledge when it comes to their right to be able to judge the credibility of the law in question. We have seen lives destroyed by a jury who was not fully informed or was informed inaccurately from the bench as to what their role is in the case. The juror controls the result solely, and they are the only person the courts are required to answer to.

Resources:

http://www.nysd.uscourts.gov/jury_handbook.php?id=10

https://www.lawyers.com/legal-info/criminal/criminal-law-basics/deliberations-in-the-jury-room.html

http://www.nysd.uscourts.gov/jury_handbook.php?id=13

http://www.courtswv.gov/public-resources/jury/juryhdbk.htm

https://www.americanbar.org/content/dam/aba/migrated/publiced/practical/books/family/chapter_14.authcheckdam.pdf

10 COMBATING A CORRUPT LEGAL SYSTEM WITH JURY NULLIFICATION

"When one gets in bed with government, one must expect the diseases it spreads."
— Ron Paul

It is more than evident that our legal system is being affected by corruption more and more each year. Corrupt law enforcement officials together with immoral judges are destroying our legal system from its core, and it is the taxpayer who ultimately suffers. One of the only peaceful ways to fight against this abuse of power by our current legal system is through jury nullification.

While there is much talk about state nullification of unconstitutional acts by the federal government popping up in mainstream media over recent years, jury nullification is a topic that is rarely heard of even among strong constitutionalists and state's rights supporters who oppose federal overreaching. As we begin informing more of the public about the importance of jury nullification, we can only hope that we see drastic changes in the legal system.

Jury nullification is a response to unlawful government behavior at times where the government incorrectly and unjustly applies the law to a criminal defendant's conduct. In the course of a criminal investigation or prosecution, the government commits an objectionable offense, and the jury punishes the government by acquitting the defendant. Jury nullification in response to unjust laws consists of jury acquittals of a defendant who is otherwise guilty under a criminal statute, yet the jury disagrees with the content of the law. In these cases, the jury can determine that the law is unjust and the law should never be applied under any circumstance. In the third category of jury nullification—jury nullification in response to inappropriate application of the law—

the jury can acquit a guilty defendant because application of the law is believed to be unjust given the circumstances and provided evidence of the case. In these situations, the jury sees nothing wrong with the overall criminal statute. Instead, the jury is determining if the state is applying the law unjustly to the accused.

When it comes to jury nullification, what we need to remember is that a jury's decision to allow a lawbreaker to go free does not compromise the integrity of the rule of law any more than the choice of an individual police officer or prosecutor not to arrest or prosecute a lawbreaker prior to the trial.

Nullification acts a check on executive and judicial actions while providing a more democratic approach to not only the application of the law, but in the manner in which is applied. The concept of jury nullification serves as a direct reminder from the bench that one of the purposes of the jury is to reflect community values. A nullification instruction would re-emphasize to the jury, and to the actors in the entire criminal justice system, why we do not employ professional fact finders in criminal cases and why we have a constitutional right to a trial by jury. Perhaps most importantly, a carefully crafted nullification instruction would allow the community to exercise its role as overseer consciously and deliberately, rather than through fictions and surrogates.

Recently juries have targeted the behaviors of police and other criminal justice system actors and when combined with modern-day media including social media, jurors often feel at risk for repercussions for their verdicts. This increased fear for the safety of the individual or their family has prompted judges to act in the best interest of the jury and protect their identities to prevent an honest deliberation and verdict regarding the trial.

According to Fully Informed Jury Association: "*Although government officials often treat modern grand juries as if they are there merely to sit down, shut up, and rubber stamp indictments assembly line-style, today's mostly meek and obedient grand juries are a far cry from the independent and critical bodies they were in early America and before."* Sadly, modern-day juries have evolved into more of a theater prop of the justice system than actual people of conscience deciding the validity of the law and if the accused genuinely are deserving of the punishment for the crime.

Given the current state of affairs in the justice system, an anarchistic form of justice would be more honest and transparent than the current model we possess. Some may argue that we at least have some system based on precedents; however, any system that advocates against one's individual rights and liberty is a system that is corrupted and devoid of merit.

As stated by the United States Supreme Court in Duncan v. Louisiana: *"Those who wrote our constitutions knew from history and experience that it was necessary to protect against unfounded criminal charges brought to eliminate enemies and against judges too responsive to the voice of higher authority. The framers of the constitutions strove to create an independent judiciary but insisted upon further protection against arbitrary action. Providing an accused with the right trial by a jury of his peers gave him an inestimable safeguard against the corrupt or overzealous prosecutor and against the compliant, biased, or eccentric judge."*

The need for jury nullification turns out to be particularly urgent when political trials are bought and sold. In ordinary criminal trials, prosecutorial prudence tempers cruel, however constitutional, laws and holds back from prompting criminal infringement not established upon society's approval. In political trials, prosecutorial discretion ceases to create a boundary between society and the laws; the people can no longer trust the morality of the actions of the state. In cases where the government itself is the victim, and the offense is the crime of challenge to the authority of the rulers themselves, the people must exercise the discretion ordinarily residing in the office of the prosecutor.

Courts possess several methods by which they can either encourage or discourage jury nullification. An understanding of these methods deepens understanding of how courts have treated jury nullification in the past and helped to frame arguments about the validity and efficacy of jury nullification. One of the most obvious ways to encourage jury nullification is to instruct the jury that it can acquit even if the prosecutor proves the elements of a crime beyond a reasonable doubt. However, a juror's ability to be informed of this right and responsibility is usually always prevented by the courts to ensure the monopoly of authority over others remains unchallenged and in the hands of solely the government.

What we can conclude from this is that jury nullification is one of the most successful ways of fighting against oppression and corruption of our legal system. When the people refuse to flex their right to use it, they give the away their constitutional authority to the corrupted system that abuses it the most.

Resources:

https://www.thenewamerican.com/usnews/crime/item/21734-jury-nullification-miscarriage-of-justice-or-check-on-tyranny

https://digitalcommons.law.byu.edu/cgi/viewcontent.cgi?article=2890&context=lawreview

http://www.socialstudies.org/sites/default/files/publications/se/6307/630711.html

http://fija.org/2015/04/09/grand-jury-is-right-to-comment-on-speak-on-government-corruption/

http://normanbird.com/visons-of-the-future-earth-jury-nullification/

https://digitalcommons.law.scu.edu/cgi/viewcontent.cgi?article=1686&context=facpubs

https://law.justia.com/constitution/us/amendment-06/04-jury-trial.html

11 GOOD JURORS DON'T ENFORCE BAD LAWS

"An individual who breaks a law that conscience tells him is unjust, and who willingly accepts the penalty of imprisonment in order to arouse the conscience of the community over its injustice, is in reality expressing the highest respect for the law"
— Martin Luther King Jr.

Our system is full of holes. Their existence lies solely in the fact that the officials who are enforcing the laws are often also the ones freely abusing those laws. If they were the only ones who are justified in bringing the critical decisions against the accused, we as the people would be sentenced to bear that heavy burden. We, the people, are those who can change the system and we are within our rights to do that.

What we all need to know is that "the grand jury possesses an unqualified power to decline to indict— despite probable cause that alleged criminal conduct has occurred. A grand jury might exercise this power, for example, to disagree with the wisdom of a criminal law or its application to a particular defendant." (Cornell) Through this, we can conclude that the jurors in some sense have unlimited power.

Contrary to what the courts and the legal system profiteers will tell you, that conclusion is right. No one can disable the juror's the right not to enforce bad laws, nor can anyone order them to bring a decision they are not in full agreement on. This unchecked power, held inside the hands of the jury, is why jurors need to exercise the rights that protected and obligated to them.

The juror has the right not only to judge the objective facts as it pertains to the trial at hand but the very law itself — a right that reinforces the importance and structure of the jury system as a check on government power. The main idea of this doctrine is that ordinary citizens, not government officials, make the final decision as to whether a person should receive punishment or not. If we are allowing the law enforcement officials and judges to enforce the laws in the manner they want to, then we would be excluded from the system, and they would decide over our fate without any restriction.

The jury was never designed to be merely a sounding board to test the adequacy of the proof placed before them, nor is it restricted to that fundamental, though vital, purpose today. The grand jury indeed adds value is through its capacity to practice vigorous circumspection not to prosecute where reasonable justification in any case exists. A grand jury might nullify the law in reaction to a criminal law that the members of the jury discover in opposition to their understanding of justice or outside the sovereign's criminalization power.

For example, members of a grand jury in the 1800s who shared the same conviction that each individual possesses a right to education might have nullified the law and prosecution of a person violating immoral laws against teaching slaves to read regardless of the amount of evidence against the accused. Likewise, a grand jury might determine that a criminal statute violates the Constitution and refuse to indict the accused under that law. Of course, the easiest way for the jurors to oppose the enforcement of bad laws is through jury nullification. It is probably the most influential weapon jurors have in their hands. Without it, the people would have no chance to oppose the system peacefully. What we need to know is that when the juror nullifies some wrong decision, he is just doing his job as it was intended to be.

Kirsten Tynan, executive director of the Fully Informed Jury Association, stated: *"Everyone in the system has discretion. Police decide whether they're going to arrest someone for a particular offense. Prosecutors decide whether or not they will charge someone for a particular offense, and what charges they are going to level. Judges even have discretion inside the courtroom, to a certain degree, and they can sometimes overturn guilty verdicts if they believe that verdict was unjust. Where the buck stop is with the jury. When they deliver a not guilty verdict, that cannot be overturned and they cannot be punished for delivering that verdict, no matter what their reason was."*

What every single juror needs to know is that their job is not based on judging whether there is doubt when a law has been violated, but rather the law was just to be applied to the people to begin with. For jurors, these are not privileges; rather these are their rights.

Once selected for jury duty, nobody will inform you of your power to judge both law and fact. In fact, the judge's instructions to the jury may be to the contrary. If you feel the laws about any criminal case on trial before a jury is wholly unfair or unjust, or that it infringes upon the defendant's inalienable or Constitutional rights, you can nullify and state that the offending statute is no law at all. Any violation of the unjust law is not a crime; for no man is required to obey an unjust edict from their government. If the accused has disobeyed some arbitrary criminal statute, and the statute is unfair and not worthy of enforcement, the defendant has in essence, committed no crime. Jurors, having decided that the justice of the law involved and opposed in either whole or certain parts of the statute to their natural understanding of what is an individual right, are obligated to the acquittal of the accused.

If we have a chance to change something unjust, we are obliged to do just that. If a juror has a chance to nullify some decisions that are contrary to his beliefs, he needs to take that chance. No one is guilty until proven otherwise and that is why the jurors must defend their right. Refusing to protect another person rights makes everything else we do inside the political process useless.

Many of us will have a chance to sit on a jury, and because of this, we must have in the forefront our mind that we are bringing the decisions and decisions that could change the course on someone's life. That type of obligation is one we need to rethink before we make our final decision. While the judges who were sworn to protect the rights of the people will misrepresent the truth when it comes to the power of jury nullification, we must have on our mind that we are not required to enforce the laws we as individuals disagree with.

Resources:

http://www.lawschool.cornell.edu/research/cornell-law-review/upload/FairfaxGrandJuryDiscretion.pdf

https://fee.org/articles/good-jurors-nullify-bad-laws-reclaiming-the-right-of-every-juror/

https://libertasutah.org/interview/how-juries-can-refuse-to-convict-people-for-breaking-an-unjust-law/

http://thecountyguard.org/jury-duty.html

12 SUCCESSFUL COURT CASES WITH JURY NULLIFICATION

"Must the citizen ever for a moment, or in the least degree, resign his conscience, then? I think that we should be men first, and subjects afterward. It is not desirable to cultivate a respect for the law, so much as for the right."
— *Henry David Thoreau*

Recently the number of jury nullification cases has grown, and that is an excellent sign that progress is being made when it comes to educating the people about the power of jury nullification. In order to see the real power of jurors and jury nullification,

The first case we will mention is the case of Antonio Willis which is famous jury nullification case, especially in Laurens County, Georgia where Willis was facing up to five years in prison. There, a jury refused to convict Willis for selling a small amount of marijuana to an undercover police officer although there was video evidence showing the transaction. During that period of time, police in Georgia were conducting a series of operations, targeting street-level drug dealers and recruited officers from other jurisdictions to assist. According to the Atlanta Journal-Constitution, the officer assumed an accent "straight out of Cheech and Chong" and pestered Antonio Willis until he sold him a few joints. The evidence was clear: Willis sold him the requested marijuana. During the trial, the judge advised Mr. Willis that he was not required to testify in his defense and that he was subject to cross-examination by the prosecution. Mr. Willis still chose to take the stand, and after 18 minutes of deliberation, the jury came back with a verdict of not guilty, even with the evidence showing he did commit the offense.

Another very famous case is the one of Julian Heicklen. In June 2010, Julian Heicklen of Teaneck, New Jersey was found distributing pamphlets that were promoting jury nullification. Heicklen, an 80-year-old retired chemistry professor, has been crusading on this issue for many years while braving numerous arrests and suffering a vast amount of abuse. His flyers were distributed outside the Federal Court in Manhattan while the contents of the pamphlets urged the potential jurors to go after their conscience in cases they disagreed with the law or government's stance. Since the pamphlets contained the statement "Juries were instituted to protect citizens from the tyranny of the government", U.S. District Judge Kimba Wood dismissed the indictment ruling that "The court holds that a person violates the statute only when he knowingly attempts to influence the action or decision of a juror upon issue or matter pending before that juror." As Heicklen was not addressing a specific case or issue before an active juror, the state had no grounds to penalize him for breaking these laws.

Another famous case centers around Ammon Bundy and many of his compatriots regarding their armed occupation of a national refuge that occurred in Oregon. Here, in a show of an unprecedented force of the people against the state, a jury delivered a fantastic blow to the overreaching government regarding the abuse of those using public lands. The jury acquitted the seven parties that were involved in conspiring to prevent federal workers from their doing their jobs at the Malheur National Wildlife Refuge while armed. After two weeks of prosecutors presenting their case and exhibiting the over 25 firearms used in the siege of Federal lands, the jury surprised everyone with a vote of not guilty, thus discrediting the government's claims. No second trial was pursued; however, Bundy was required to return to his home state of Nevada regarding the armed standoff from a few years prior.

Dr. Jack Kevorkian's case is another example of jury nullifying a bogus charge against someone. Kevorkian, known in the 90's as the "Mercy Doctor", felt that it was immoral for the government to force someone to live in pain and fought for the right of his patients to die with dignity. Going against the edicts of the state, Dr. Kevorkian developed a system that allowed people with terminal illnesses to end their life peacefully and humanely. The state, opposed to euthanasia for humans, attempted to convict Dr. Kevorkian on multiple counts of murder stating he had no right to help others die. Even though he admitted to assisting numerous people in ending their life, the jury found him not guilty of the crime of murder and nullified the law in that situation.

As it pertains to jury nullification for marijuana-related crimes, no other name echoes more than that of New Jersey Weedman, Ed Forchion. Best known for his involvement in the legalization of marijuana movement, Forchion has not been a stranger to being arrested for marijuana-related crimes. As he is has been diagnosed with bone cancer, the New Jersey Weedman led the charge on using marijuana as an alternative to highly addictive opiate-based painkillers in a state that did not recognize marijuana as a viable treatment for chronic pain. Arrested for possession and intent to distribute, Forchion represented himself in court and crafted arguments in a way that promoted empathy from the jury. He also was able to inform them about their right to jury nullification and how they are able not just to judge the facts of the case, but the validity of the law as well. At the end of the proceedings, the jury nullified the law in this case and acquitted him of all charges. This case didn't stop the state for again arresting Forchion for another marijuana-related charge in 2014.

These cases act as a recent testimonial of situations where the jury holds more power than the courts in matters where the law is outdated or immoral and prohibits the rights of the individual to act in a manner that is not genuinely criminal. As the state continues to restrict and deprive people the ability to be free, fail-safes built into our judicial process allows for the people to stand opposed and remind the government who exactly is in control of the system. When lawmakers enact draconian laws that go against the rights of the people and the courts enforce these same oppressive laws, the people hold the ultimate say over if these laws are to be exercised.

Resources:

https://www.criminallegalnews.org/news/2018/feb/16/jury-nullification-crucial-check-government-power/

http://www.peachtreenorml.org/end-prohibition/case-jury-nullification-rural-georgia

http://infomory.com/famous/famous-jury-nullification-cases/

https://www.msn.com/en-us/news/us/jury-acquits-leaders-of-oregon-standoff-of-federal-charges/ar-AAjuxZf

http://paradigmsanddemographics.blogspot.com/2018/01/the-case-for-jury-nullification-parts-i.html

https://danieljmitchell.wordpress.com/2018/01/10/the-case-for-jury-nullification-part-i/

https://jacksnavelyjurynullification.weebly.com/famous-cases.html

ABOUT THE AUTHOR

Liberty enthusiast, advocate, and co-host of the popular liberty based podcast "Uncivil Liberty", Luke von Trapp is actively engaged in liberty based action through media, education, and community involvement inside Alabama, one of the most liberty-adverse states in the United States.

Starting back in 2010, Luke began his workings inside the political realm by working in talk radio where he spent his time fighting for liberty against the illogical rantings of both conservatives and liberals. Since the formation of the podcast "Uncivil Liberty", Luke and the UL team have been able to advance the conversation of liberty based action into the state of Alabama and beyond.

When Luke isn't busy with irritating intellectually dishonest people on every side of the aisle while advocating for liberty, he prefers to spend his time with his friends and family while working on the family farm.

Printed in Poland
by Amazon Fulfillment
Poland Sp. z o.o., Wrocław

57327097R00040